I Can Do It!

# I Can Swim

By Meg Gaertner

**www.littlebluehousebooks.com**

Copyright © 2023 by Little Blue House, Mendota Heights, MN 55120. All rights reserved. No part of this book may be reproduced or utilized in any form or by any means without written permission from the publisher.

Little Blue House is distributed by North Star Editions:
sales@northstareditions.com | 888-417-0195

Produced for Little Blue House by Red Line Editorial.

Photographs ©: Shutterstock Images cover, 7, 11 (top), 11 (bottom), 12–13, 15 (top), 15 (bottom), 16–17, 19, 20–21, 24 (top left), 24 (bottom left), 24 (bottom right); iStockphoto, 4, 8–9, 22–23, 24 (top right)

**Library of Congress Control Number: 2022901675**

**ISBN**
978-1-64619-580-0 (hardcover)
978-1-64619-607-4 (paperback)
978-1-64619-660-9 (ebook pdf)
978-1-64619-634-0 (hosted ebook)

Printed in the United States of America
Mankato, MN
082022

## About the Author

Meg Gaertner enjoys reading, writing, dancing, and being outside. She lives in Minnesota.

# Table of Contents

I Can Swim **5**

Glossary **24**

Index **24**

# I Can Swim

I take a swimming class.

I learn from a teacher.

The teacher holds me up.

I feel the water
around me.

I swim safely.

I swim only if an adult
is around.

I wear goggles.

They protect my eyes.

I wear floaties.

They keep me

above water.

I lie on my back.

The water holds me up.

I'm floating!

floating

I kick my legs underwater.

I paddle my arms.

I stay in one place.

underwater

I reach one arm forward.

I pull it through the water.

Then I use my other arm.

I'm swimming!

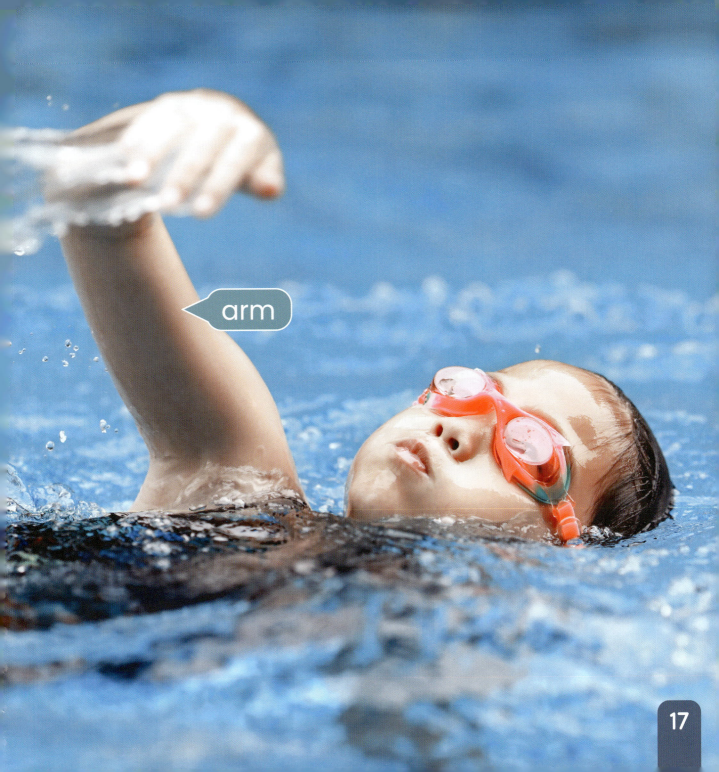

I swim across the pool.

I reach the side.

I have a big smile.

I know how to leave
the water.
I find a ladder.
I climb up.

I walk to the diving board.

I jump into the water.

I make a big splash!

# Glossary

**floaties**

**splash**

**goggles**

**underwater**

# Index

**F**
floating, 12

**G**
goggles, 10

**L**
ladder, 20

**T**
teacher, 5-6